# STAR WARS®

# A MUSICAL JOURNEY
## EPISODES I–VI

## MUSIC BY JOHN WILLIAMS
## ARRANGED BY TOM GEROU

EXCLUSIVELY DISTRIBUTED BY

HAL•LEONARD®

ISBN-13: 978-0-7390-6650-8

# CONTENTS

# 20TH CENTURY FOX FANFARE

Composed by **Alfred Newman**
Arranged by Tom Gerou

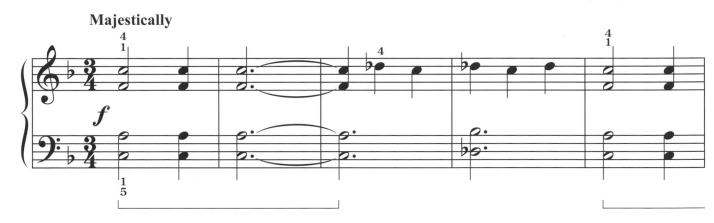

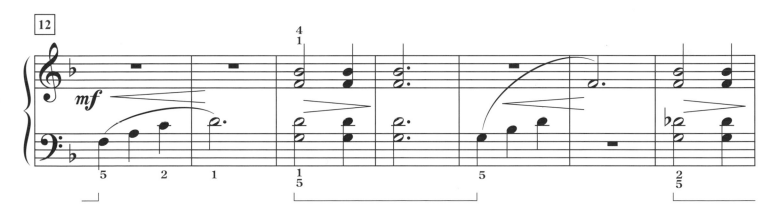

# STAR WARS
## (Main Title)

Music by JOHN WILLIAMS
Arranged by Tom Gerou

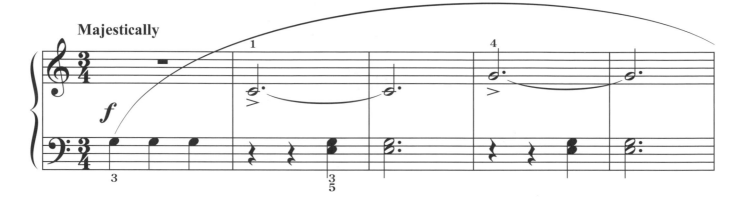

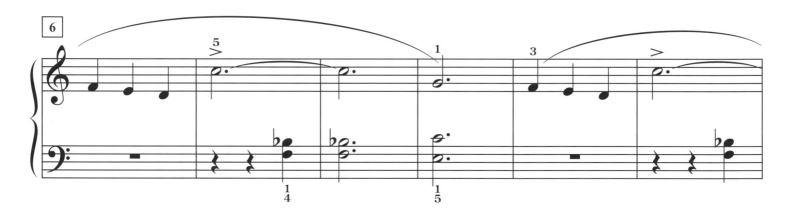

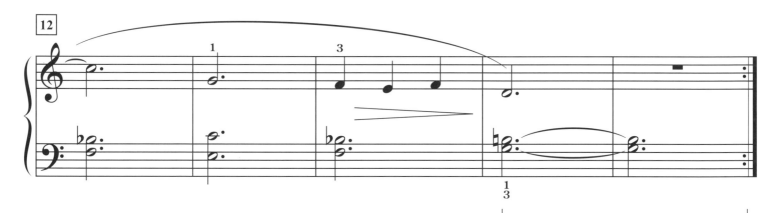

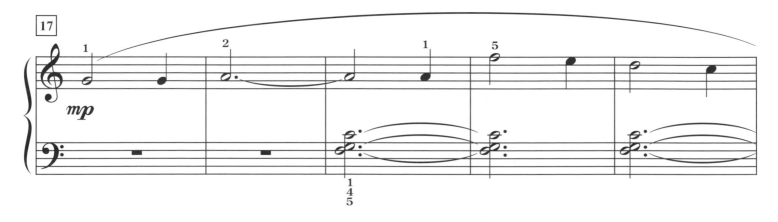

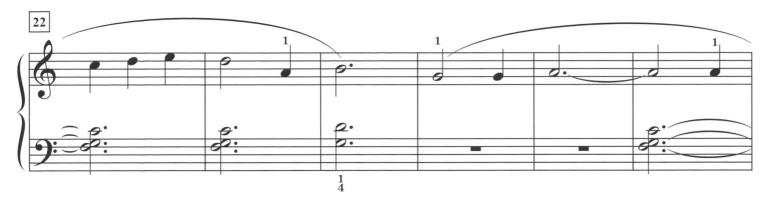

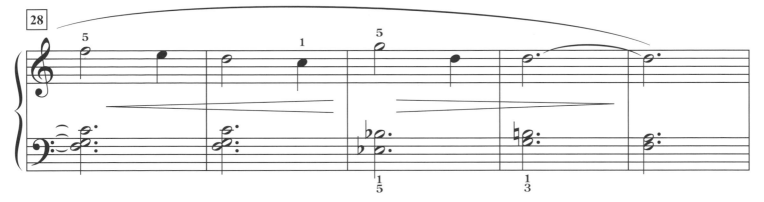

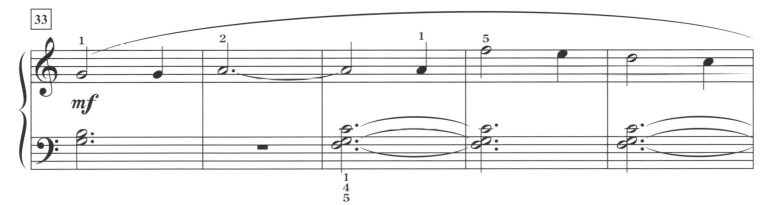

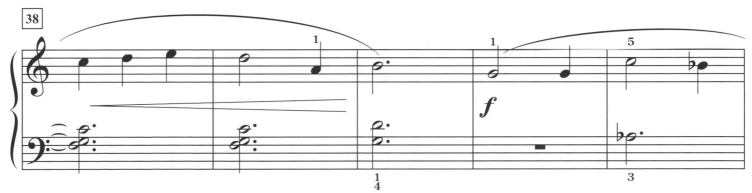

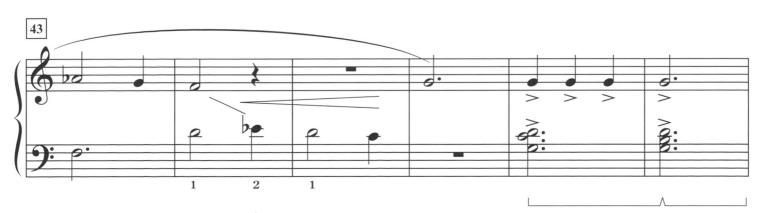

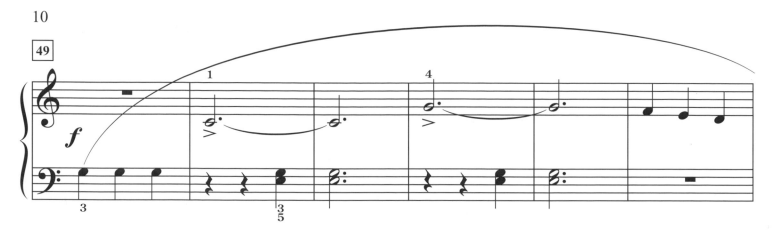

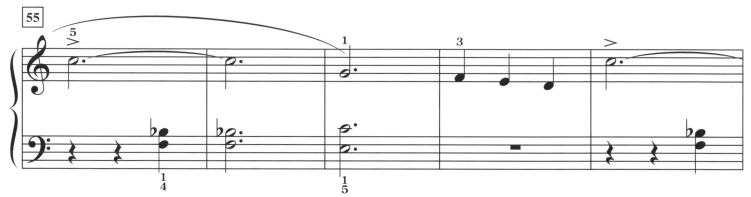

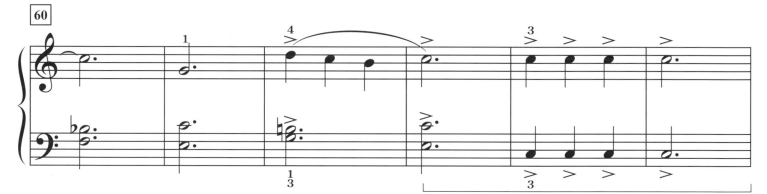

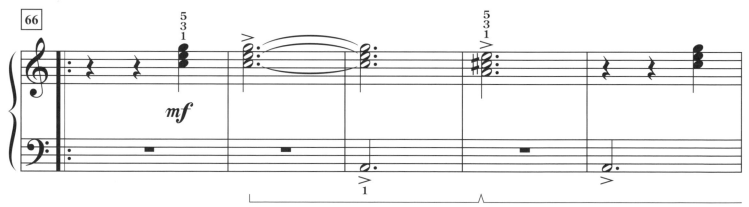

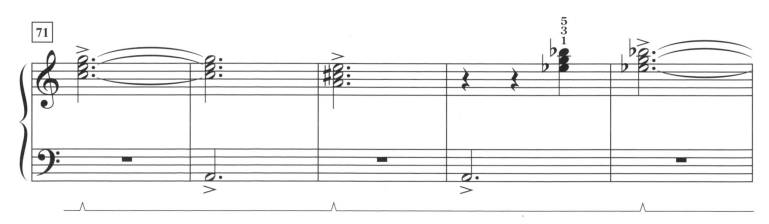

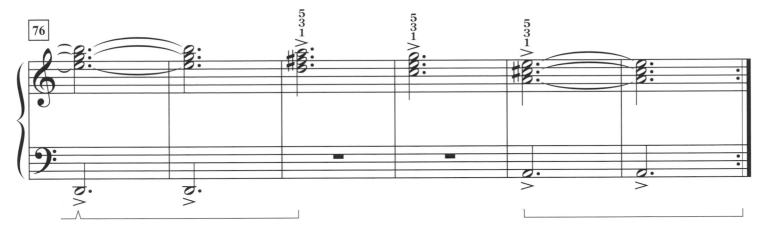

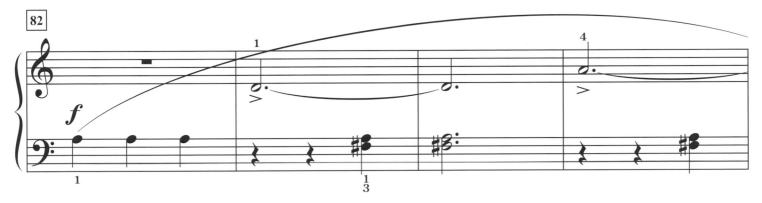

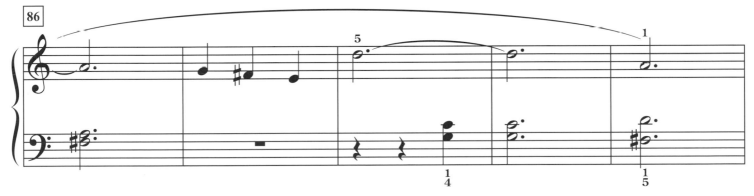

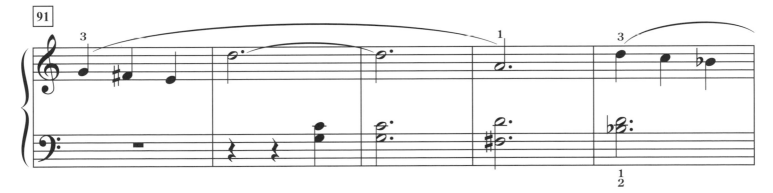

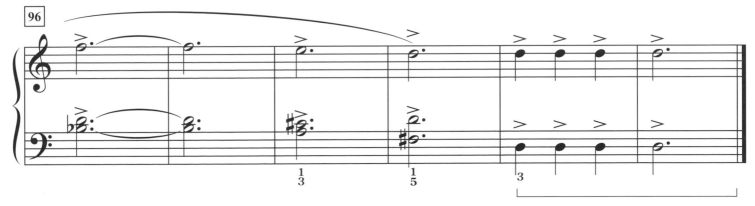

# DUEL OF THE FATES

Music by **JOHN WILLIAMS**
Arranged by Tom Gerou

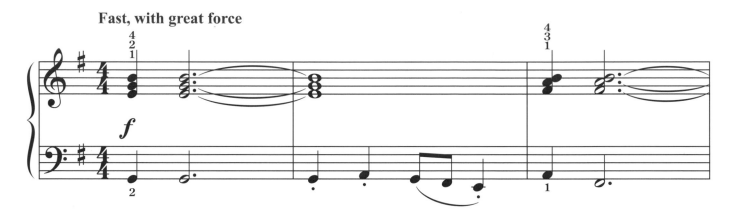

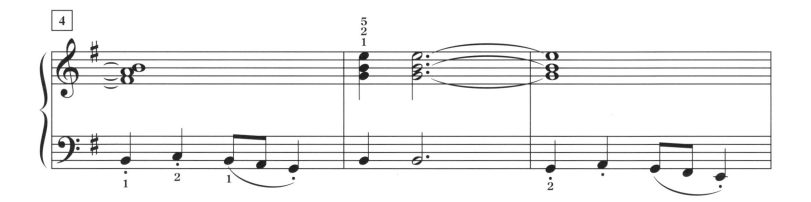

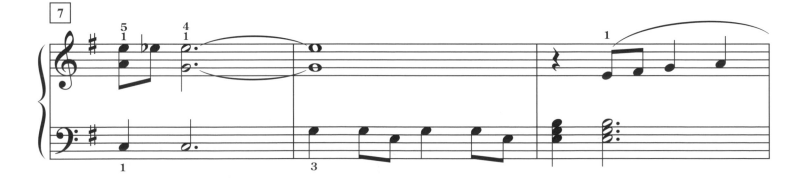

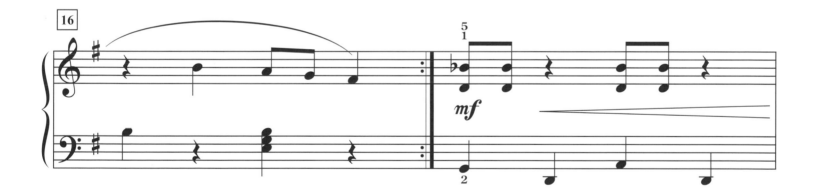

# ANAKIN'S THEME

Music by **JOHN WILLIAMS**
Arranged by Tom Gerou

Moderately slow

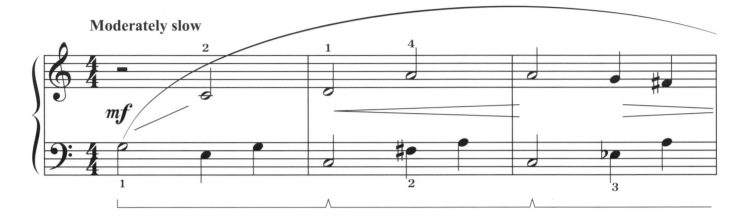

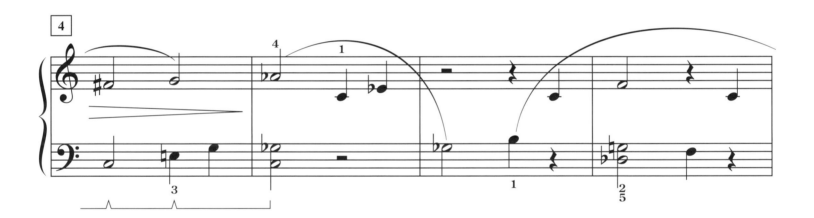

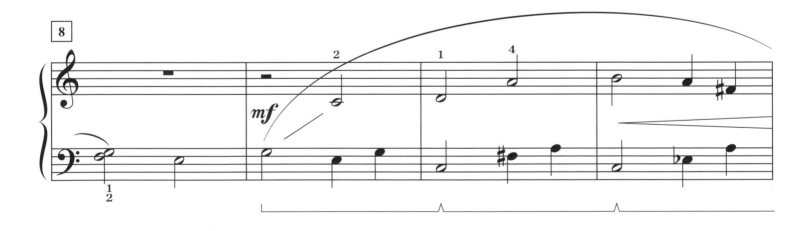

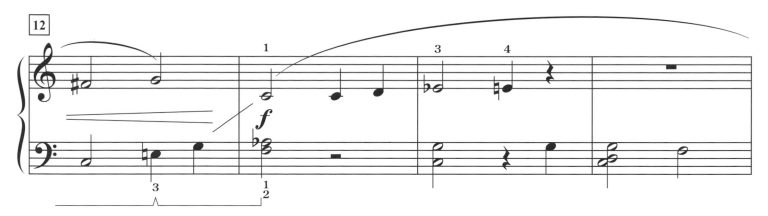

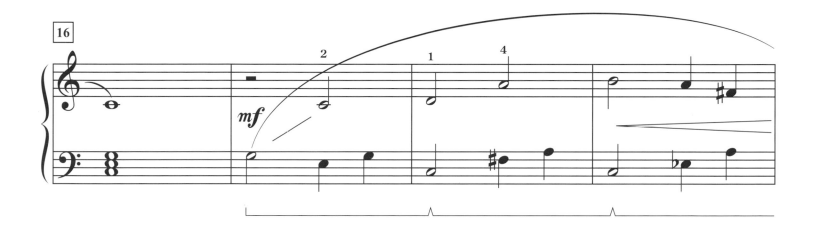

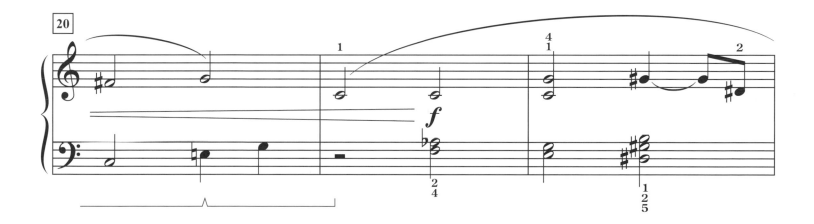

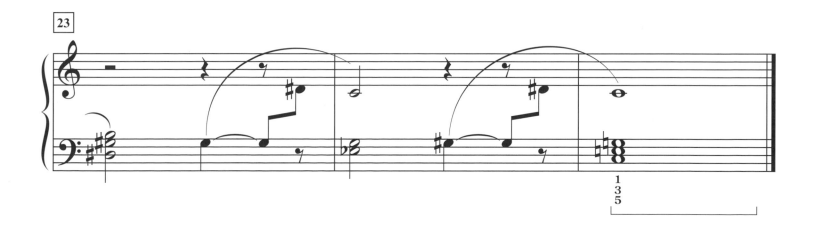

# YODA'S THEME

Music by **JOHN WILLIAMS**
Arranged by Tom Gerou

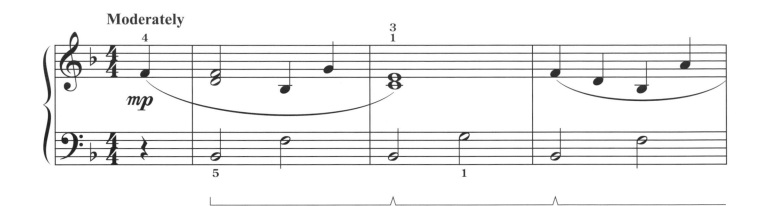

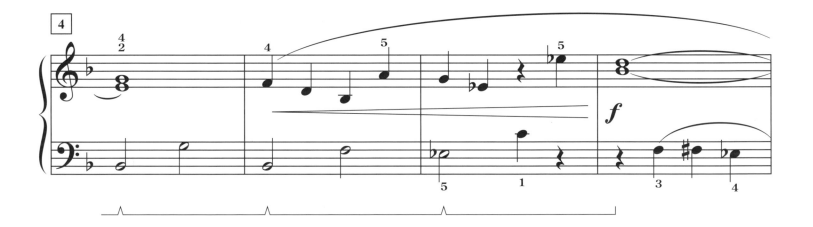

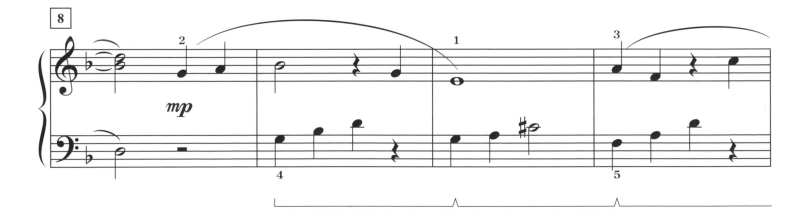

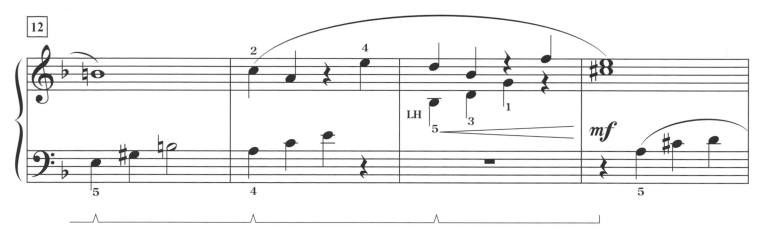

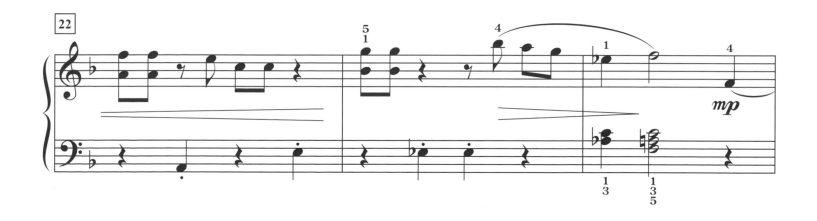

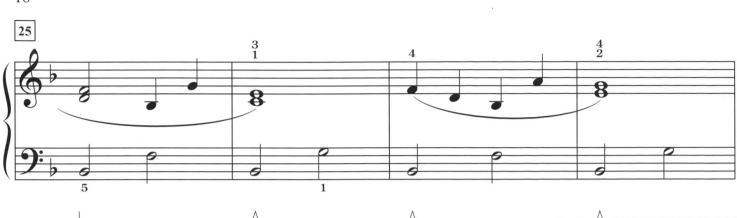

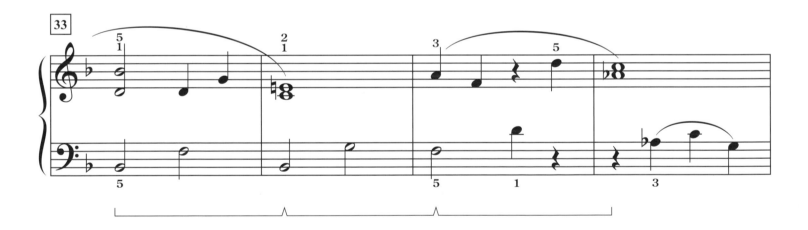

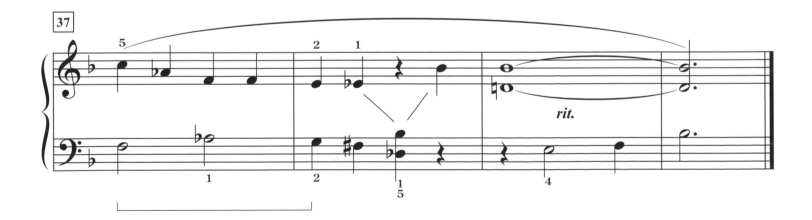

# ACROSS THE STARS
## (Love Theme)

Music by JOHN WILLIAMS
Arranged by Tom Gerou

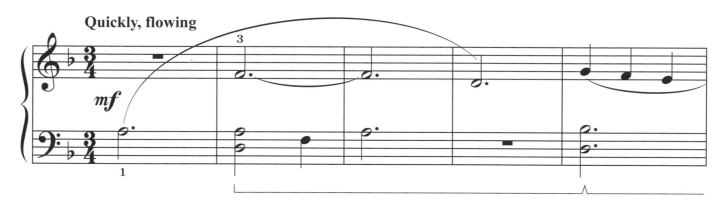

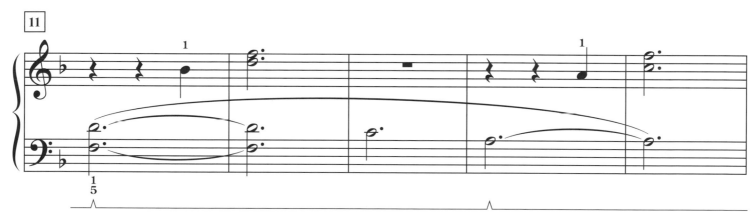

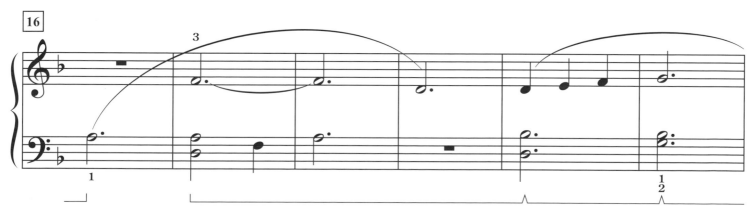

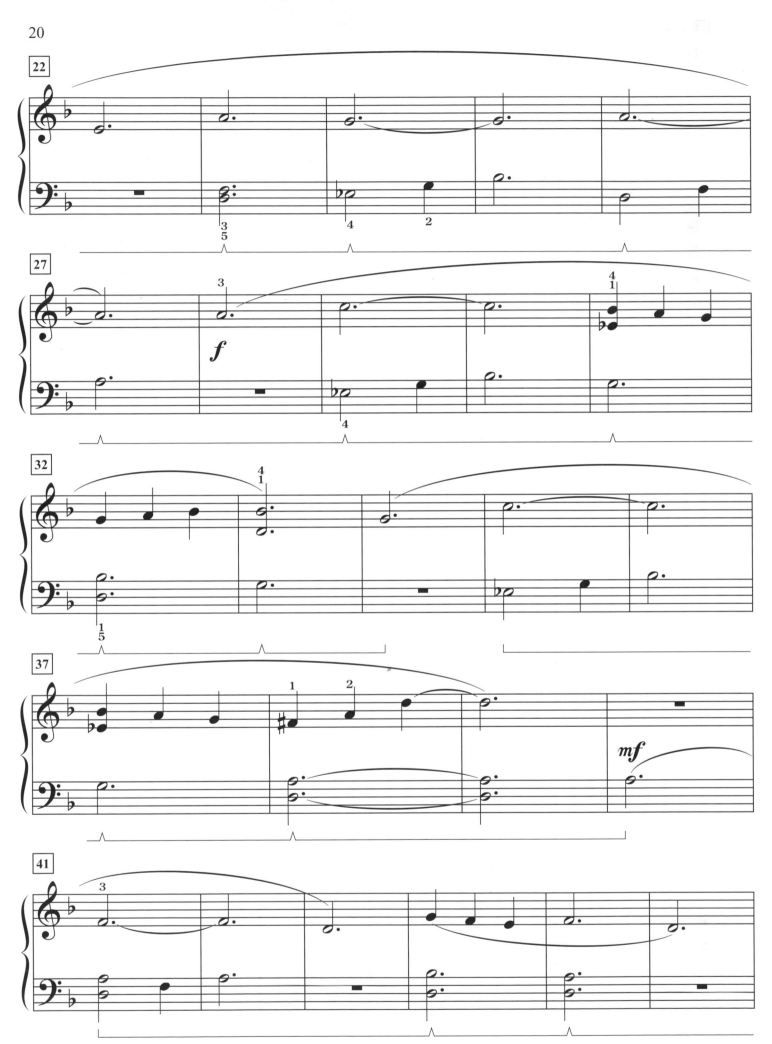

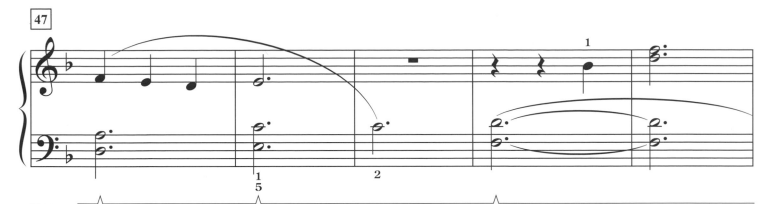

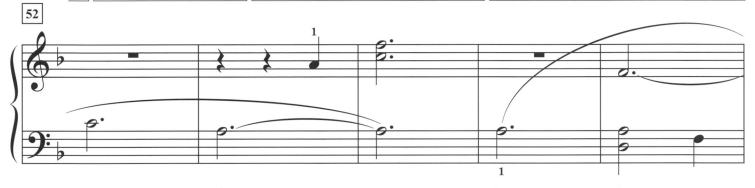

# BATTLE OF THE HEROES

Music by **JOHN WILLIAMS**
Arranged by Tom Gerou

**Maestoso, with great force**

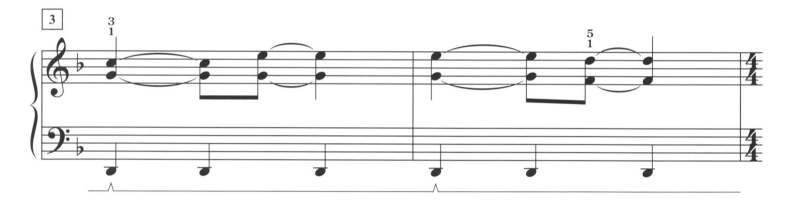

23

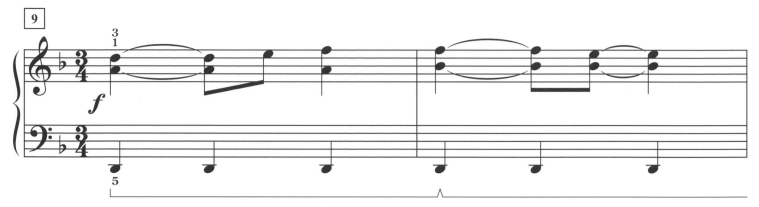

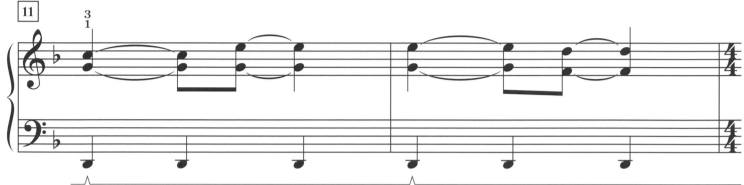

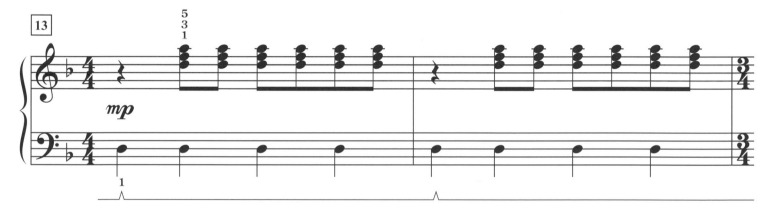

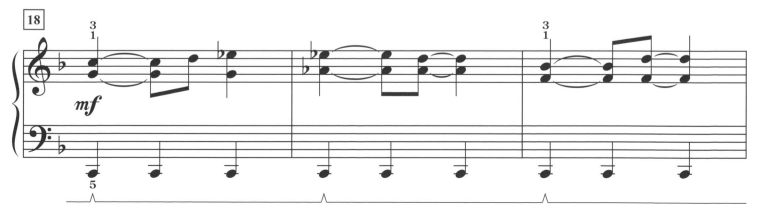

24

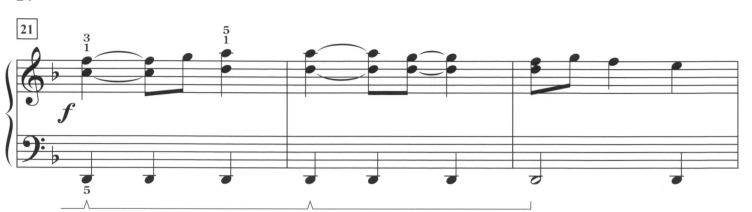

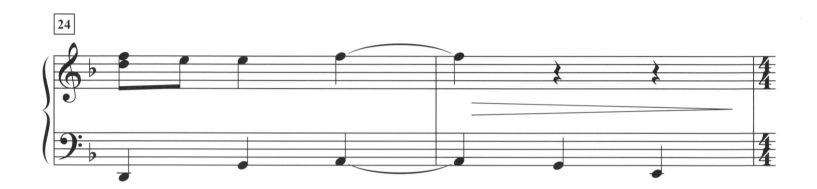

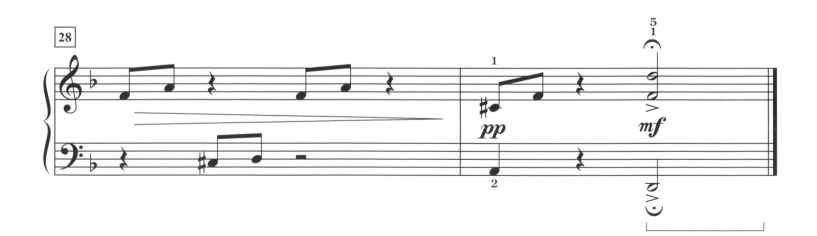

# CANTINA BAND

Music by **JOHN WILLIAMS**
Arranged by Tom Gerou

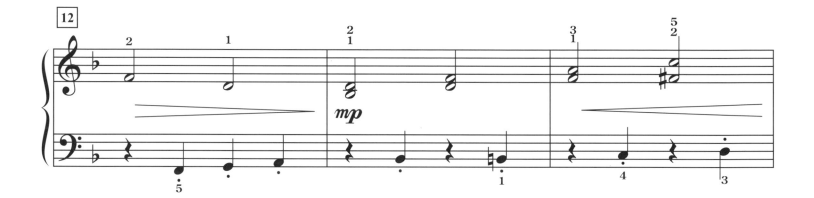

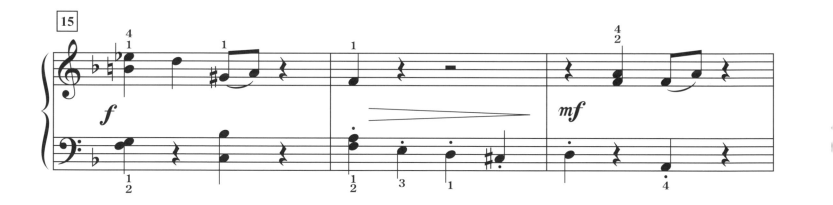

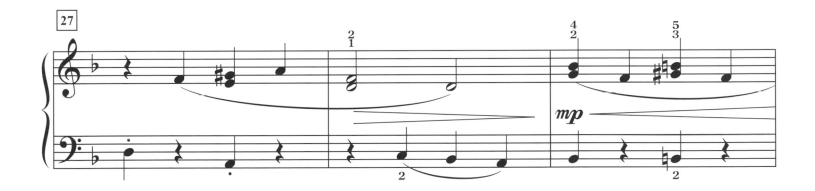

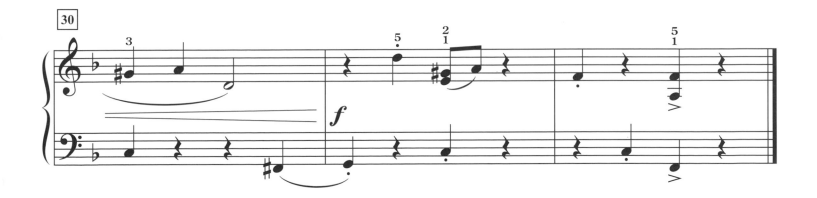

# THE IMPERIAL MARCH
## (Darth Vader's Theme)

Music by **JOHN WILLIAMS**
Arranged by Tom Gerou

Steady march tempo

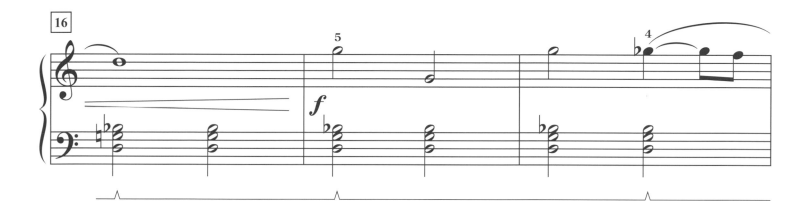

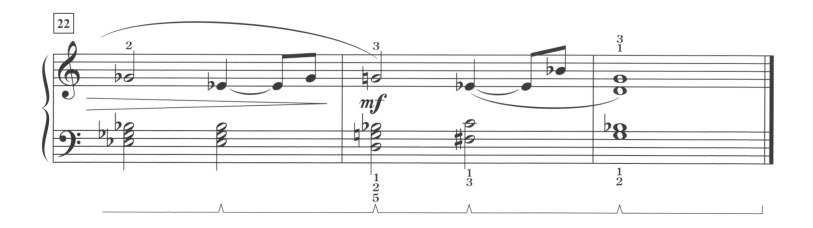

# MAY THE FORCE BE WITH YOU

Music by **JOHN WILLIAMS**
Arranged by Tom Gerou

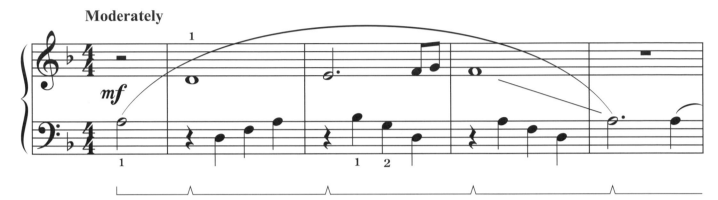

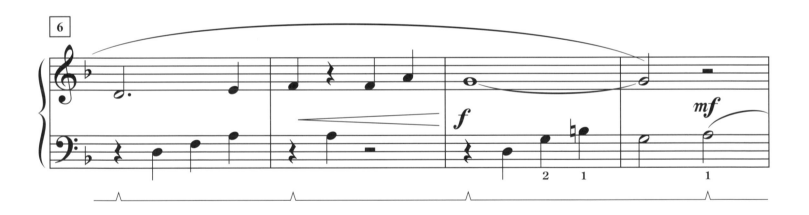

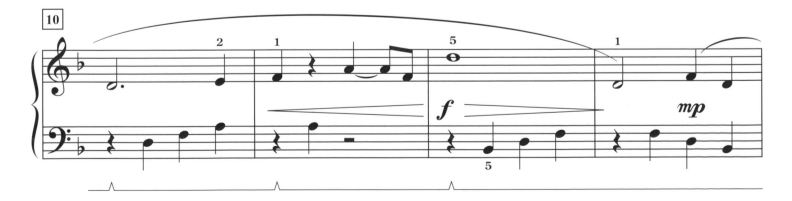

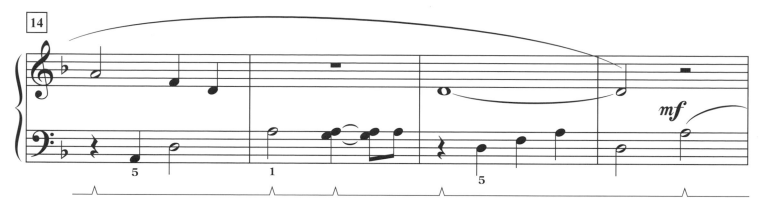

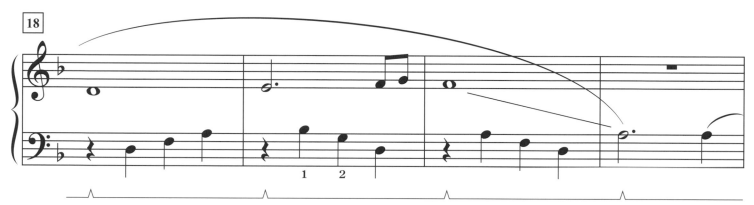

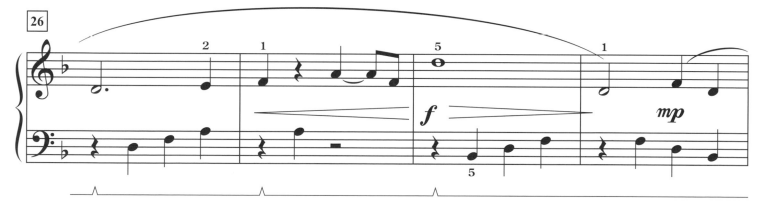

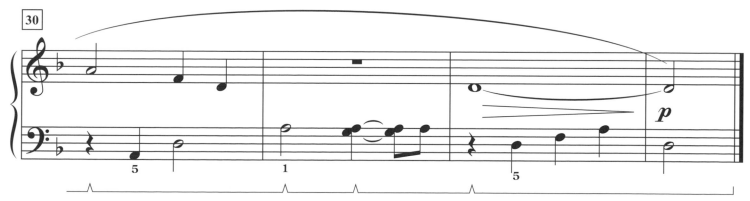

# LUKE AND LEIA

Music by **JOHN WILLIAMS**
Arranged by Tom Gerou

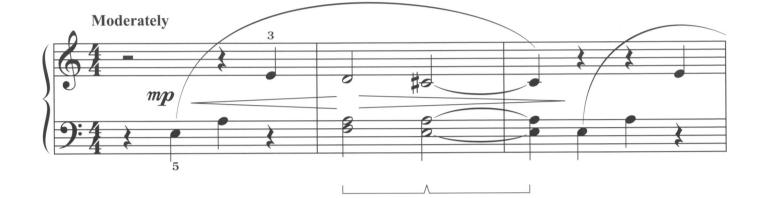

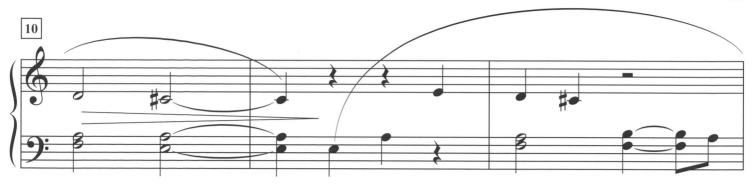

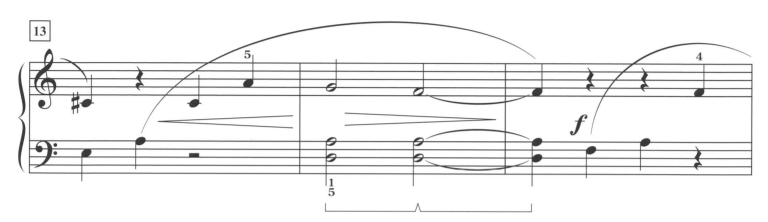

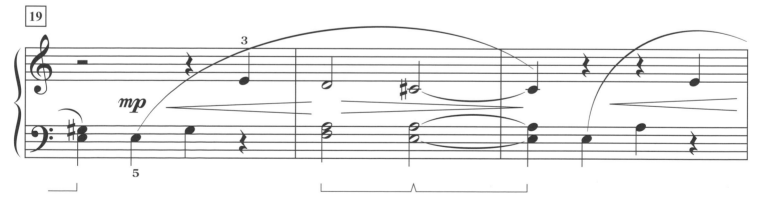

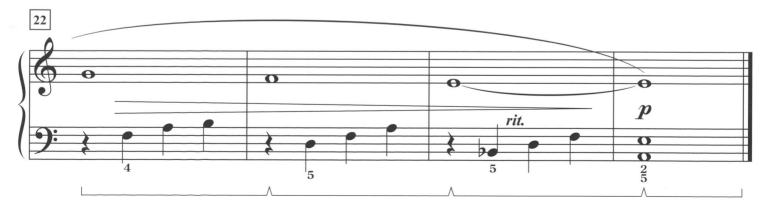

# JAWA SANDCRAWLER

Music by **JOHN WILLIAMS**
Arranged by Tom Gerou

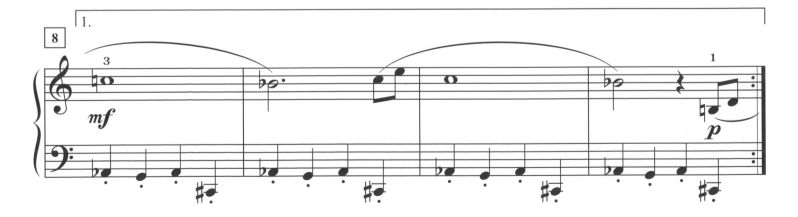

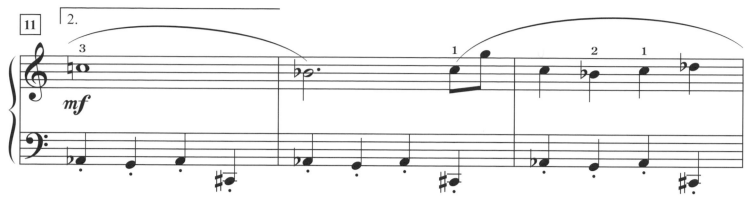

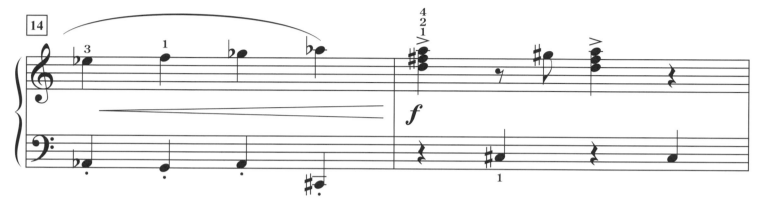

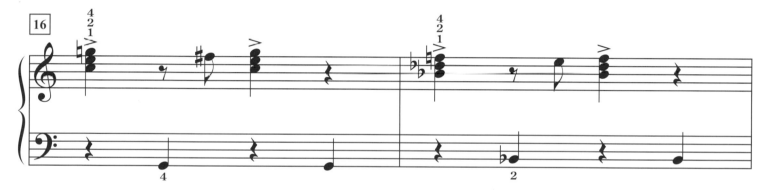

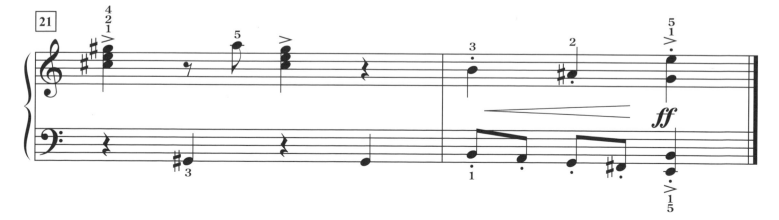

# BINARY SUNSET

Music by **JOHN WILLIAMS**
Arranged by Tom Gerou

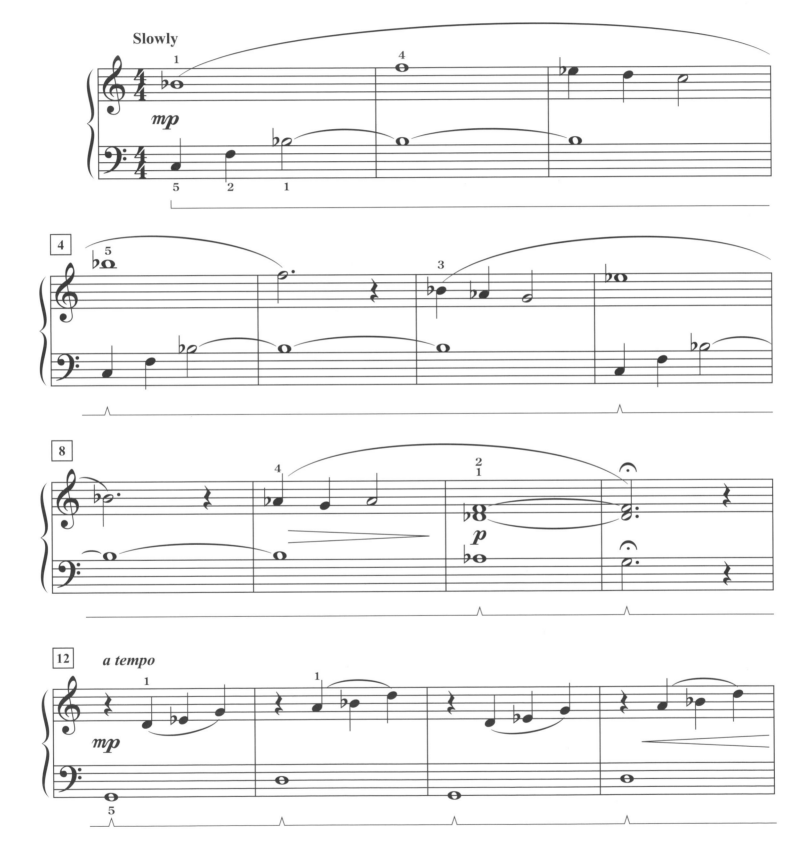

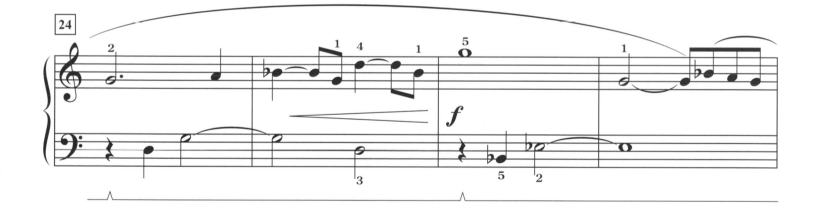

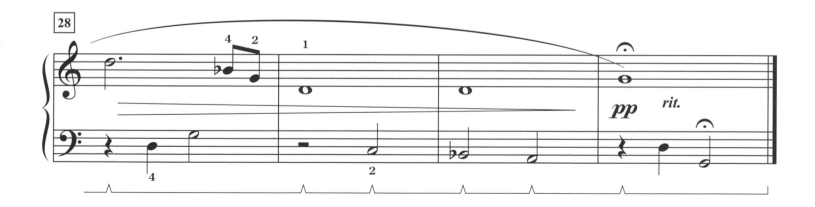

# THE THRONE ROOM

Music by JOHN WILLIAMS
Arranged by Tom Gerou

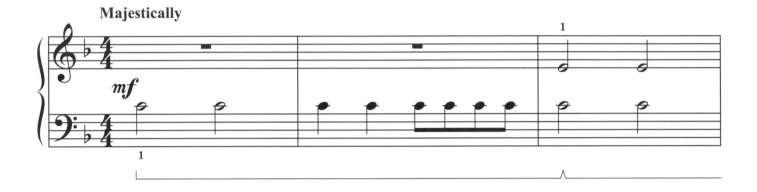

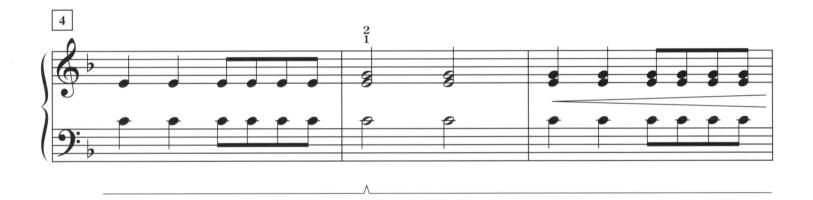

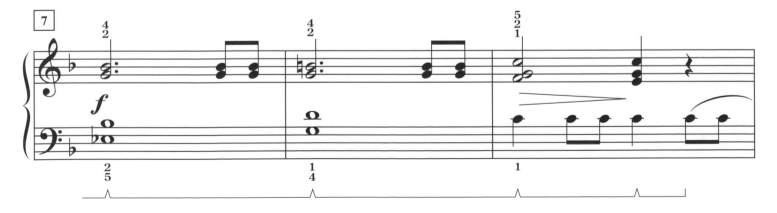

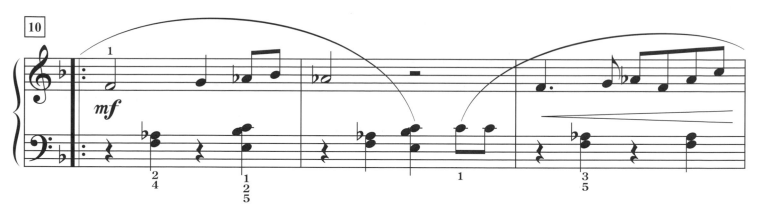

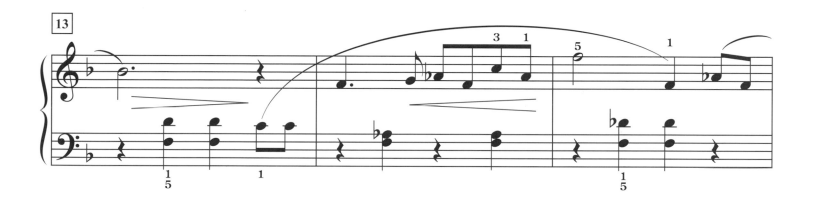

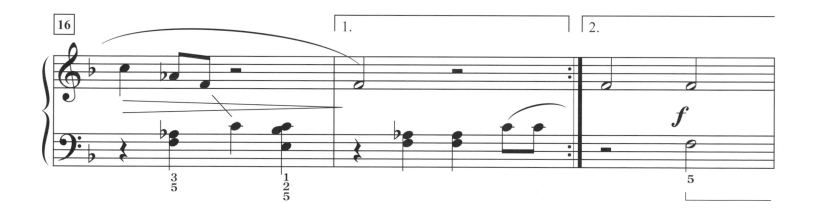

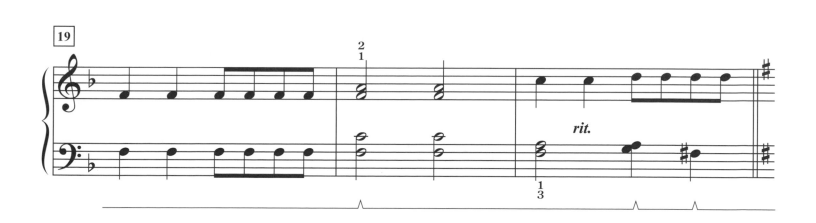

**22** **March tempo**

**25**

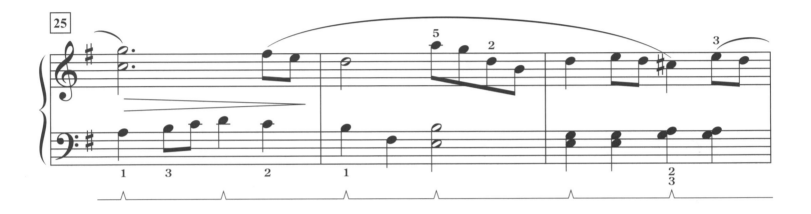

**28**

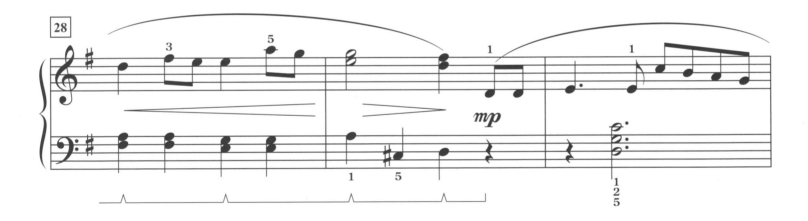

**31**

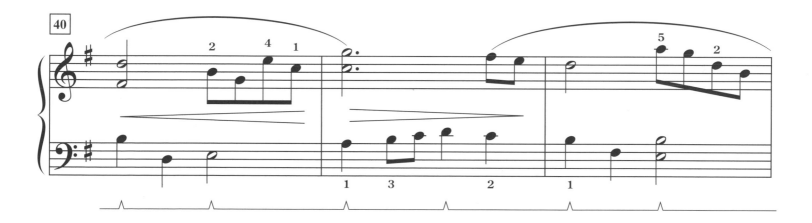

# PRINCESS LEIA'S THEME

Music by **JOHN WILLIAMS**
Arranged by Tom Gerou

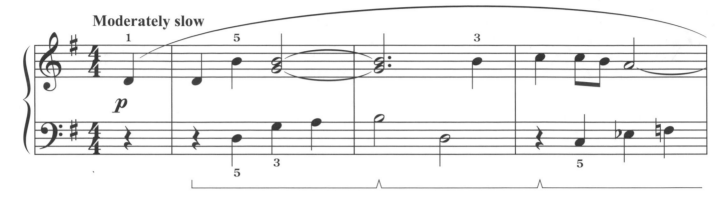

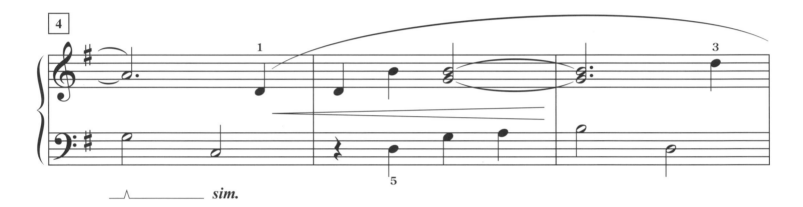

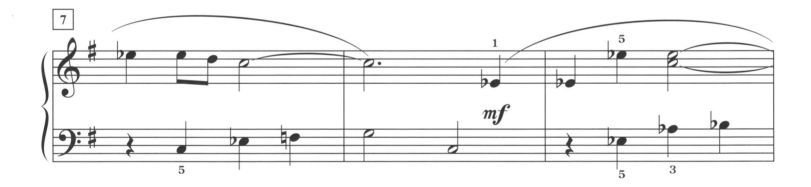

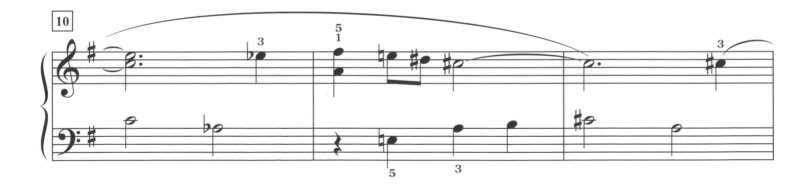

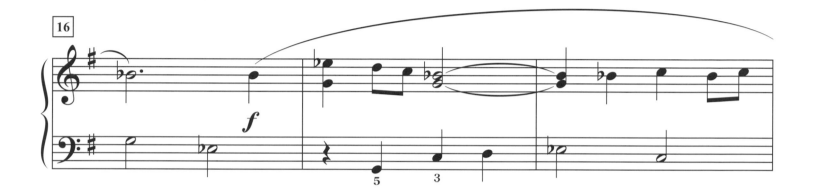

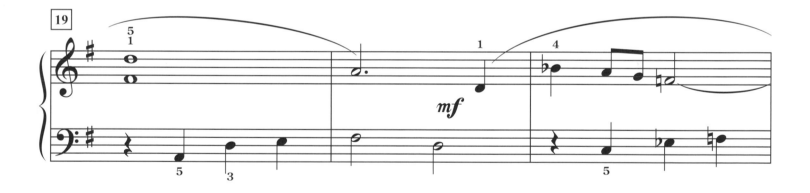

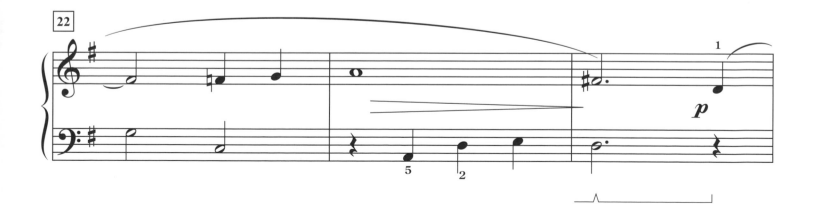

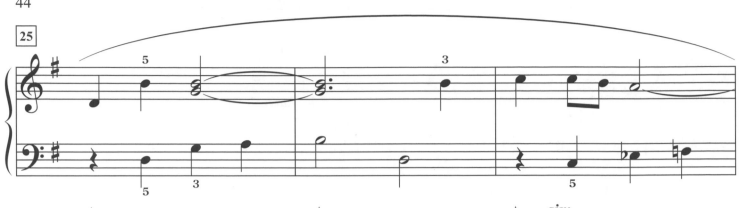

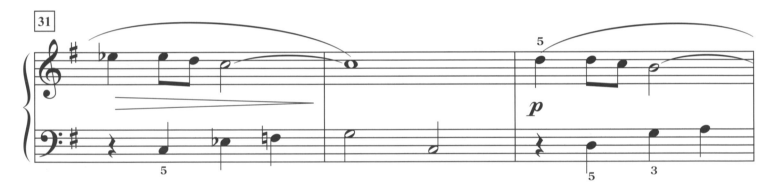

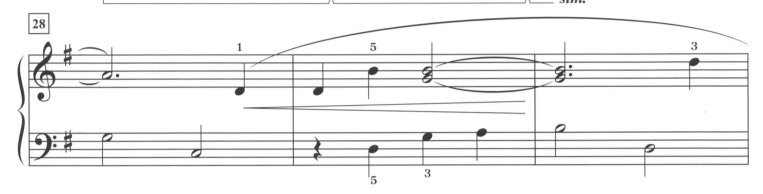

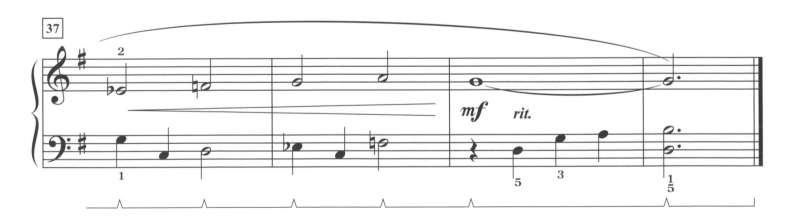